FOUND!

BRONZE AGE

Moira Butterfield

W
FRANKLIN WATTS
LONDON•SYDNEY

Franklin Watts
First published in Great Britain in 2017 by The Watts Publishing Group

Credits
Series Editor: John C. Miles
Series Designer: Richard Jewitt
Picture researcher: Diana Morris
Picture Credits: Anteromite/Shutterstock: 1 bg, 30-31 bg, 32 bg. Sabena Jane Blackbird/Alamy: 17c. Matt Cardy/Getty Images: 22-23. Chris Collyr. stone-circles.org.uk 11. Cranach/Shutterstock: front cover t. cynoclub/Shutterstock: 16b. C M Dixon/Topfoto: 13tr. Vladimir Floyd/istockphoto: 15tr. ifong/Shutterstock: 17br. Kletr /Shutterstock: 16br. Thomas Lenne/Shutterstock: back cover br. lowephoto/Alamy: 25tr. LuFeeTheBear/Shutterstock: front cover bg. David Lyons/Alamy: 27. A Dagli Orti/DEA/Getty: 9tr. PAS/CC wikimedia commons: back cover tl. Photolibrary Wales/Alamy: 9. Photoshot: 27tr. Geoff Robinson/Rex Shutterstock: 24-25. Skyscan/Alamy: 29tr. Tzido Sun/Shutterstock: 17tr. udra11/Shutterstock: front cover bg c. Rui Vieira/PAI: 23tr. Robin Weaver/Alamy: 10-11. Wessex Archaeology: 4, 5, 7l, 7r, 19c, 19tr, 20-21, 21tr. WHA/Alamy: front cover main, 13. WHA/Topfoto: 1c, 28-29. Gary Young/Dartmoor National Park Authority, www.dartmoor.gov.uk : 14-15.

HB ISBN 978 1 4451 5294 3
PB ISBN 978 1 4451 5295 0

Printed in China

Franklin Watts
An imprint of
Hachette Children's Group
Part of The Watts Publishing Group
Carmelite House
50 Victoria Embankment
London EC4Y 0DZ

An Hachette UK Company
www.hachette.co.uk

www.franklinwatts.co.uk

CONTENTS

Bringer of metal
AMESBURY ARCHER

Around 4,300 years ago, the secrets of making metal came to Britain from Europe, beginning a period of history we call the Bronze Age. Before this time people in Britain lived in a time we call the Stone Age, when most tools were made from flint (a type of stone). One of the earliest people ever to make metal in Britain was found buried in Amesbury, not far from the circle of stones called Stonehenge.

Around
2,300 BCE

EARLY
BRONZE AGE

DATE FOUND:
MAY 2002,
BY ARCHAEOLOGISTS DIGGI
ON A BUILDING SITE.
THE SITE IS NOW
A SCHOOL.

PLACE FOUND:
AMESBURY,
WILTSHIRE.

As archaeologists were digging on a building site they found the grave of a very unusual man. In his grave there were some small gold objects, the earliest gold so far found in Britain. He also had a cushion stone, which was used in the process of metal-making. He was aged between 35 and 45 when he was buried. Scientists could tell by analysing his teeth that he grew up somewhere near Switzerland, so he must have travelled to Britain.

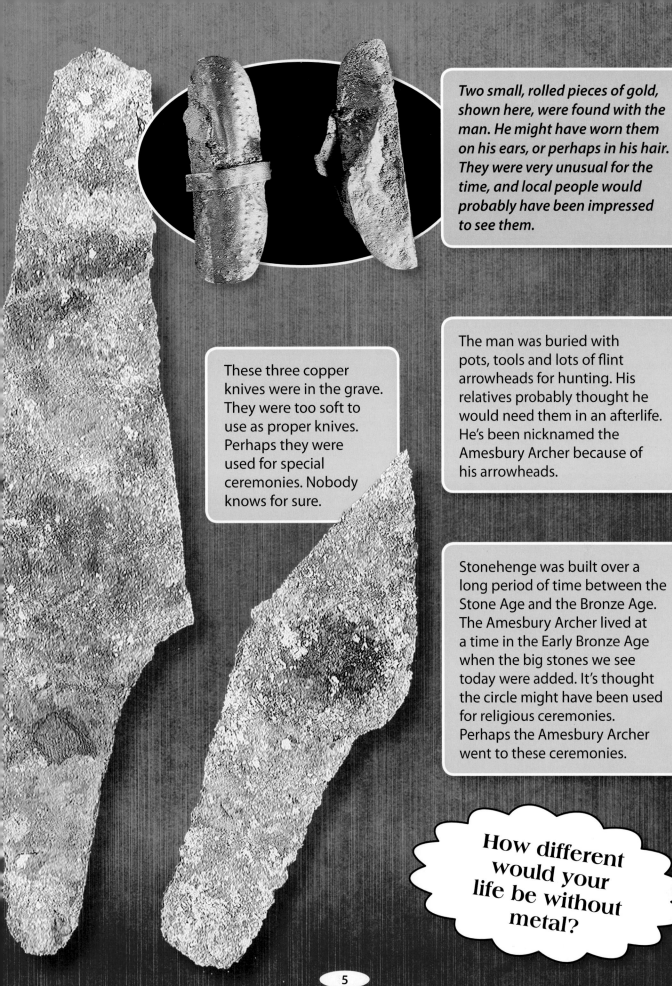

Two small, rolled pieces of gold, shown here, were found with the man. He might have worn them on his ears, or perhaps in his hair. They were very unusual for the time, and local people would probably have been impressed to see them.

These three copper knives were in the grave. They were too soft to use as proper knives. Perhaps they were used for special ceremonies. Nobody knows for sure.

The man was buried with pots, tools and lots of flint arrowheads for hunting. His relatives probably thought he would need them in an afterlife. He's been nicknamed the Amesbury Archer because of his arrowheads.

Stonehenge was built over a long period of time between the Stone Age and the Bronze Age. The Amesbury Archer lived at a time in the Early Bronze Age when the big stones we see today were added. It's thought the circle might have been used for religious ceremonies. Perhaps the Amesbury Archer went to these ceremonies.

How different would your life be without metal?

Clues to solve
BOSCOMBE BURIALS

People had no written language in Bronze Age Britain, so they did not write anything down. We can only discover clues about them by looking at the objects they left behind and studying their burial remains. Lots of Early Bronze Age burials have been found at Boscombe Down, near Stonehenge, and the finds there give us a glimpse into life 4,000 years ago.

2,300 BCE -1,400 BCE EARLY BRONZE AGE

DATE FOUND:
2003 – BOSCOMBE BOWMEN.
2005 – BOY WITH THE AMBER NECKLACE.

PLACE FOUND:
BOSCOMBE DOWN, WILTSHIRE.

In 2003, workers putting in a new water pipe at Boscombe Down found a grave containing the jumbled bones of seven people buried at different times. There were three men, a teenage boy and three children, along with arrowheads, tools and pots. In 2005, roadworks unearthed the nearby burial of another teenage boy and a very unusual necklace. The grave objects provide clues that Early Bronze Age people travelled round Britain and Europe.

The men in the grave were nicknamed the Boscombe Bowmen because of the arrowheads buried with them. It's thought possible they were part of community of Stonehenge builders living close to the site of the stone circle. Perhaps they should be nicknamed the Boscombe Builders instead.

Analysis of the Boscombe Bowmen's teeth showed they didn't grow up locally. They probably came from Wales. We know that some of the Stonehenge stones came from Wales, too. That's why some think the men might be Stonehenge builders.

Alongside the bones there were eight clay pots, decorated with lines made by cord being wrapped round the wet clay. One of the pots was decorated with plaited cord. That's a good Bronze Age clue! Pots decorated with plaited cord came from elsewhere in Europe, so this pot probably came by boat from abroad.

The teenage boy found in 2005 was wearing a necklace of 90 beads made of Danish amber. It would have been rare and precious. Analysis of the boy's teeth provided a big surprise. He came from somewhere near the Mediterranean Sea! We'll never know why he was near Stonehenge when he died.

What is your most valuable possession and where was it made?

Making metal
GREAT ORME

Bronze is made by heating copper and tin and mixing them together. In the Bronze Age it was used to make axes, swords and daggers. Nobody knew where Britain's Bronze Age copper supply came from until a huge, hidden copper mine was rediscovered. We know the date of the mine because the miners left some of their Bronze Age tools behind.

Around
1,800 BCE
-800 BCE
EARLY TO LATE
BRONZE AGE

DATE FOUND:
1987, WHEN A CAR PARK WAS BEING PLANNED.

PLACE FOUND:
LLANDUDNO, CLWYD, WALES.

A piece of Welsh wasteland was earmarked for a car park in 1987, but plans changed when cavers discovered the Great Orme Mine, an incredible nine kilometres of underground tunnels. They were littered with thousands of ancient stone hammers and antler tools, once used to chip at the rock. The miners had hand-chipped all the tunnels to get to copper ore – rock containing copper. During the Bronze Age they took enough copper from Great Orme to make up to 10 million bronze axe heads.

It would have been tough work chipping out the rock on hands and knees in the freezing darkness. Some of the tunnels at Great Orme are so narrow it's thought that small children must have worked in them.

Once miners collected the copper ore it was brought to the surface. The rock fragments were heated up over a charcoal fire to separate out the copper. Hot liquid copper was poured into moulds to make bars called ingots.

A Bronze Age metalworker would heat a copper ingot along with some tin to make glowing, hot liquid bronze. It was poured into a clay mould shaped like an axe head, dagger or sword. When the metal cooled, the mould was broken to get to the object inside.

The oldest bronze object ever found in Britain was a dagger buried with a Bronze Age fighter who had been killed by sword blows. He died around 2,200 BCE and was buried in a field near Chichester. A similar dagger, found in Italy, is shown above.

At the heart of the mine there is a big chamber, shown here, completely hand-chipped out of the rock. It is the largest man-made chamber so far discovered in the world.

What metal tools do you use in your home? What metal they are made of?

Mystery messages
GARDOM'S EDGE STONES

The Bronze Age Britons have left behind lots of mysteries we can only guess at. For instance, though they did not write down language they did leave some carved shapes on rocks. People have different ideas about what the carved patterns mean. What do you think?

2,300 BCE
-1,500 BCE
EARLY
BRONZE AGE

DATE FOUND:
1965, BY AN
EAGLE-EYED
ARCHAEOLOGIST.

PLACE FOUND:
NEAR BASLOW,
DERBYSHIRE.

The person who spotted the carving on a boulder at Gardom's Edge had found something incredibly rare – a message left by someone in the Bronze Age! The stone at Gardom's Edge is so precious that it was buried out of sight soon after it was found, to keep it safe. An exact replica was placed in the original location. Spiral rock patterns like this are found on rocks in Scotland, Ireland and northern England, too.

This type of carving is called 'cup and ring' because the pattern of rings goes round a small cup shape. Rock carvings like this are called petroglyphs.

It's possible that spiral carvings like this mark a route to somewhere important, perhaps a sacred place where lots of travellers went. An upright stone, called a standing stone, was put near the carving. It must have marked something, too, but we don't know what.

It's also possible the carved spiral shapes meant something magical to people in the Bronze Age, though we can't know for certain what they thought.

This standing stone was put up at Gardom's Edge. Bronze Age standing stones like this are found all over Britain. They mark something, but what? We'll never know!

Bronze Age carvers sometimes made rock carvings of axe shapes as well as spirals. Laser scans of the famous Stonehenge stones have revealed lots of axe head carvings and a dagger shape carved into the stones. The carvings have worn down over the years, so only scans can detect them.

Can you imagine living without any written words?

Buried treasures
MOLD CAPE

In Early Bronze Age Britain, a group of people emerged who had extra wealth and importance compared to others. They were probably important leaders and their families. They were buried differently from ordinary people, in round mounds called barrows. Sometimes they had treasures put in their graves with them. One of the greatest British Bronze Age treasures ever found, the Mold Cape, was found in a barrow.

Around
1,600 BCE
EARLY
BRONZE AGE

DATE FOUND:
1833, BY WORKERS DIGGING FOR STONES.

PLACE FOUND:
MOLD,
FLINTSHIRE.

When workers dug into a barrow in Wales they found a stone-lined box called a cist. Inside, there were hundreds of gold fragments and beads, along with parts of a skeleton. The skeleton parts were soon lost, but the gold fragments were kept and later put together to recreate a gold cape. It would have been very valuable. It's possible that it might have belonged to someone made wealthy by the Great Orme copper mine, located nearby (see p. 8).

The cape was beaten out from a single gold ingot about the size of a table tennis ball. It would have taken a lot of skill to make it so thin and finely decorated. It was probably embellished with amber beads and lined with leather.

The cape was small and whoever put it on would not have been able to move their arms very well. Perhaps they only wore it for special ceremonies.

Several beautiful gold cups have been found in Bronze Age burial mounds, though no other cape has ever been discovered. There are over 10,000 known Bronze Age barrows around Britain, so perhaps more treasure will turn up!

A beautiful gold cup – the Rillaton Cup – was found in Rillaton Barrow in Cornwall. It is another of Britain's best Bronze Age treasures.

The Bronze Age people who were buried in mounds were wrapped in cloth and cremated (burnt) first. Then the burnt remains were put in a clay pot before being buried.

Can you imagine wearing the Mold Cape or drinking from a gold cup?

Bronze Age clothes
WHITEHORSE HILL CIST

In Britain, Stone Age people mainly wore animal skins, but by Bronze Age times they began to wear clothes made from woven materials. They made fabric by weaving sheep's wool, cow hair or plant fibres. A girl was buried with some of her clothes and jewellery around 3,500 years ago on Dartmoor in Devon.

Around **1,500** BCE

EARLY BRONZE AGE

DATE FOUND: 2013, WHEN THE GRAVE WAS EXCAVATED.

PLACE FOUND: DARTMOOR, DEVON.

The grave was first noticed by a walker on the high, wild landscape of Dartmoor. When it was excavated, the girl's cremated bones were found wrapped in fur. They had been put into a stone-lined box (cist) along with a basket of belongings. When the earth that hid the cist wore away, the end stone fell out and the grave was spotted. The excavated remains were taken to a lab and analysed using high-tech microscopes and X-rays to reveal their secrets.

In the grave there was cloth woven from nettle fibres. There was also an armband made of plaited cow hair, decorated with tin beads. It would have looked just like a modern friendship bracelet.

In the Dartmoor grave there were four, round wooden pieces that look very like ear studs of the kind worn by some people today.

There were lots of clay, stone and amber beads in the grave. They would have been threaded on a pretty necklace. The orange amber came from Eastern Europe.

British Bronze Age clothes are very rare finds, but we know from clothes found in Denmark that people wore wool tunics and leggings or long skirts and tops. They sometimes wore woolly hats and cloaks, too.

Finds from around Europe give us some more clues to Bronze Age clothes. Bronze Age woollen underwear was found in Holland and a leather handbag decorated with dog teeth was discovered in Germany!

Have you ever worn a belt, woven bracelet or necklace, just like people did 3,500 years ago?

Pottery detective work
NEWBALD FOOD POT

Food pots are sometimes found in Bronze Age burial barrows. Rather like a detective, an archaeologist can gather clues from a pot, such as the date it was made and even the type of food cooked inside it. The pot shown here is a typical example. Someone cooked in it and ate from it around 3,500 years ago.

Around
1,550 BCE

EARLY
BRONZE AGE

DATE FOUND:
1883, IN A
BARROW BURIAL.

PLACE FOUND:
NORTH NEWBALD,
EAST YORKSHIRE.

The Newbald Pot was found in Victorian times by amateur archaeologists exploring a Bronze Age barrow. We can tell from food remains found in pots like this that life was changing in Britain during the Bronze Age. People began to farm more, growing their own cereal crops and keeping farm animals to eat. In earlier times, during the Stone Age, people ate wild plants and hunted wild creatures.

The pot was made from clay and decorated with lines. The Bronze Age potter who made it would have marked it using a piece of animal bone, a bird quill or a stick. It would have been set on top of a fire to cook food.

In parts of Africa, Asia and Europe people still sometimes cook food in clay pots, just as people did in Bronze Age times.

Bronze Age farming families had to grind the wheat and barley they grew to make flour. It would have been a long, hard job to crush the cereal using heavy stones. The flour was then used to make flatbread.

Scientific analysis can be used to study the molecules left behind by food cooked in Bronze Age pots. We know from these tests that recipes included nettle stew, with added chunks of meat or fish caught from local streams. Barley and herbs were added, too.

What foods do you eat that are cooked in a pot or made with flour?

Under us now
HEATHROW AIRPORT

Hidden remains from long ago are just a few metres beneath the Earth's surface, sometimes in surprising places. For instance, it turns out that Bronze Age people lived on the land that is now under Heathrow, one of the world's busiest airports! The biggest-ever dig in the UK took place before Heathrow's Terminal 5 was built, and it uncovered Bronze Age farms.

Around
1,500 BCE

EARLY TO MIDDLE
BRONZE AGE

DATE FOUND:
2002—2003, ON A
15-MONTH DIG.

PLACE FOUND:
HEATHROW AIRPORT,
MIDDLESEX.

Eighty archaeologists searched one million square metres of land before Heathrow Terminal 5 was built. They found nearly 9,000 years of history, and 80,000 objects! Some of the Bronze Age finds they discovered were preserved in a damp waterhole, including the wooden bowl shown here.

The wooden bowl was a very rare find. Wood usually rots away, but the bowl was preserved because it lay in damp earth. Amongst other finds there was a Bronze Age spearhead and a ring made from a spiral of copper.

The dig revealed that people were starting to divide land up, using ditches, banks and hedgerows. They were beginning to develop their own farms; owning their own territory instead of sharing the land.

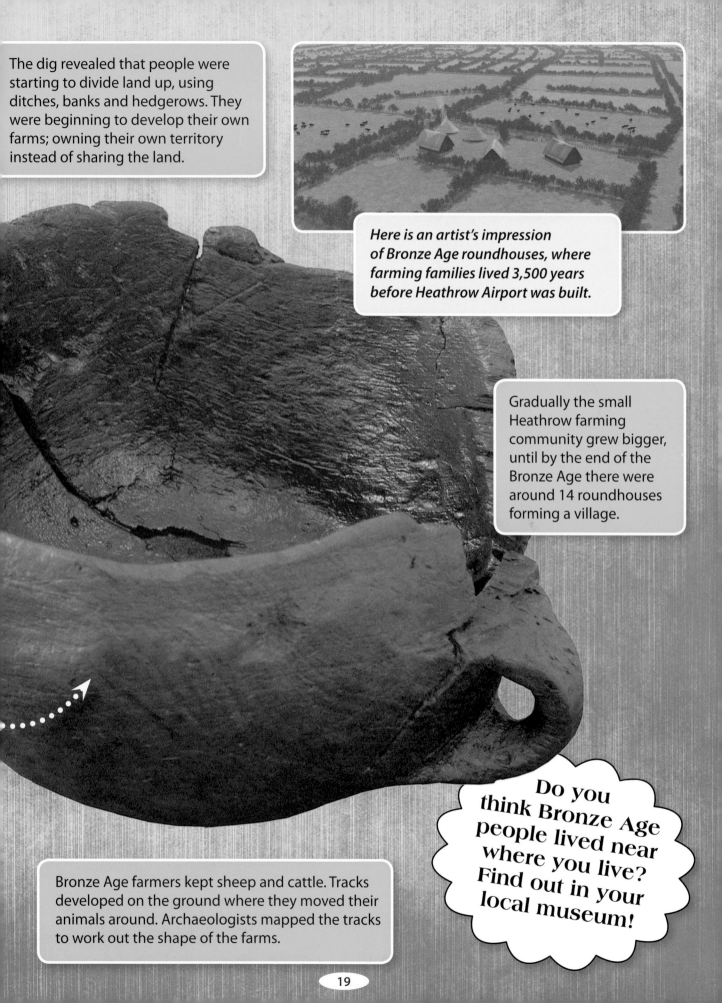

Here is an artist's impression of Bronze Age roundhouses, where farming families lived 3,500 years before Heathrow Airport was built.

Gradually the small Heathrow farming community grew bigger, until by the end of the Bronze Age there were around 14 roundhouses forming a village.

Bronze Age farmers kept sheep and cattle. Tracks developed on the ground where they moved their animals around. Archaeologists mapped the tracks to work out the shape of the farms.

Do you think Bronze Age people lived near where you live? Find out in your local museum!

A buried beast
KINGSMEAD QUARRY

By the Middle Bronze Age people's lives had changed a lot. They no longer moved around following wild animal herds, as Stone Age people once did. Now they were more settled and they began to believe in different things, too. Archaeologists discovered a strange secret in a quarry near Windsor that provides a clue to their beliefs.

1,400 BCE - 1,100 BCE MIDDLE BRONZE AGE

DATE FOUND: DIG STARTED 2003.

PLACE FOUND: HORTON, NEAR WINDSOR, BERKSHIRE.

Archaeologists began hunting for finds in Kingsmead Quarry before it was dug for gravel. They discovered two Middle Bronze Age farms, with fields and animal paddocks. On one of the farms, nine farm animals were carefully buried in pits around the site. Amongst them was the calf shown here. It's thought the animals might have been buried as an offering to Bronze Age gods to persuade them to keep the farm safe.

This calf was deliberately buried in its own pit. There were eight cattle and one sheep buried in all, each in their own hole.

The farmers who lived at Kingsmead would have wanted their farm animals and crops to do well. They probably thought that by offering something, perhaps to the spirits of the Earth, they stood a better chance of having a good year on the farm.

As well as cattle, the farmers buried a pot with food inside it as an offering. The pot was still marked with soot from a cooking fire that burned 3,500 years ago.

This picture shows an archaeologist excavating a big clay pot from Kingsmead Quarry. It might have been used by Bronze Age farmers for storage.

Imagine keeping your own animals and crops for food, with no shops to buy food from.

Bronze Age farming families could store some food during the winter, but if they had a bad year on the farm their food supplies might run out and they could even starve. Life would have been tough for them.

Time to travel
PETERBOROUGH BOAT FLEET

The easiest way to travel around Britain and Europe in the Bronze Age was by boat. We know that Bronze Age people were skilled boat builders because a few examples have been found. About 3,000 years ago, somebody deliberately sank a fleet of eight Bronze Age boats in the East of England. In 2011 they were rediscovered, still in amazing condition.

Oldest boat
1,600 BCE
Newest boat
1,000 BCE
MIDDLE BRONZE AGE

DATE FOUND:
2011, BY ARCHAEOLOGISTS

PLACE FOUND:
WHITTLESEY, CAMBRIDGESHIRE.

In 2011 a local archaeologist noticed a few interesting pieces of wood sticking out from a quarry face near Peterborough. Soon it became clear that the timbers were Bronze Age, so more investigations began and the boats turned up nearby. They had been sunk in an old river creek and they were preserved in the waterlogged mud. Someone had deliberately taken the transom from each boat. A transom is a piece of wood that stops water coming in through the back.

The biggest boat found at Whittlesey was nearly 9 m long. We know that big Bronze Age boats were able to sail over to Europe, with up to 18 rowers on board. This picture shows a reconstruction of a large Bronze Age boat at the National Maritime Museum in Falmouth.

One of the Whittlesey boats was decorated inside and out with a pattern that looked like noughts and crosses. Another was fitted with oak handles for pulling it out of the water. Several had been repaired with clay patches.

The boats were probably used by fishermen in the local streams and lakes. One of the boats had traces of a cooking fire on board, used to cook a fish catch. Archaeologists found a funnel-shaped basket nearby, used to trap eels.

Once the boats were excavated they were sprayed with water for months to carefully get rid of dirt and grime but keep them from drying out. Once cleaned (above), they were soaked in a special wax to help preserve them. The boats are on display at Flag Fen Archaeology Park in Cambridgeshire.

We can't tell why the Whittlesey boats were sunk. Perhaps someone wanted to hide them and come back to get them later, but never did. Perhaps they were sunk as some sort of religious offering.

Imagine only being able to travel by boat or by foot. Could you manage?

Watery World
MUST FARM

1,000 BCE -700 BCE LATE BRONZE AGE

In 2016, archaeologists announced they had found a Late Bronze Age settlement hidden deep beneath the watery fens of Cambridgeshire, very close to the fleet of boats featured on p. 22. The homes had lain undisturbed for 3,000 years until they were discovered in a clay quarry. They tell a dramatic story of a fiery disaster.

DATE FOUND: DISCOVERED IN 2006 BUT EXCAVATED IN 2015–2016.

PLACE FOUND: WHITTLESEY, CAMBRIDGESHIRE.

Experts think there were probably five houses at Must Farm. They were built on a wooden platform standing on stilts over a river. One day a fire ripped through them and they collapsed into the water below, where mud helped to preserve them.

We don't yet know how the fire started. If there was an attack, evidence might one day be found. One human skull has been found so far, but we don't yet know if it was someone who died on the day of the fire.

This picture shows an archaeologist uncovering the earliest complete wheel in Britain, found alongside the homes. It was about a metre wide and made of wood. The people who lived at the Must Farm site were very good carpenters.

The families had to escape the fire so quickly they left behind their meals. There was even a wooden spatula left in a pot. When the fire struck it was being used to stir pottage, a type of porridge flavoured with herbs.

The houses at Must Farm were roundhouses, similar to this reconstruction at Flag Fen Archaeological Park in Cambridgeshire. A roundhouse would have been dark and smoky inside, with a cooking fire in the centre. Everyone lived together in one room.

Rare Bronze Age fabric was found at the site, along with cups, bowls, beads and even a little wooden box. The fabric was woven from bark fibres gathered from a lime tree.

Can you imagine what it would have been like living in a roundhouse along with your family?

water treasure
LOCH GLASHAN

In the Late Bronze Age people began to throw valuable treasures into rivers and lakes, especially weapons. It's thought they were probably making ritual offerings, perhaps to bring themselves good luck. Some of these Bronze Age river treasures have been rediscovered, including a dagger and swords thrown into Loch Glashan in Scotland.

1,000 BCE
-700 BCE
LATE
BRONZE AGE

DATE FOUND: 1979, BY A SCHOOLGIRL WALKING ALONG THE SHORE.

PLACE FOUND: LOCH GLASHAN, ARGYLL.

Short daggers like this are called dirks in Scotland. A local schoolgirl noticed this Bronze Age dirk under a stone by the side of the Loch. The mud around it had worn away, and she became the first person to see it since it was thrown into the Loch 3,000 years ago. Long, thin Bronze Age swords called rapiers have also turned up in the same Loch.

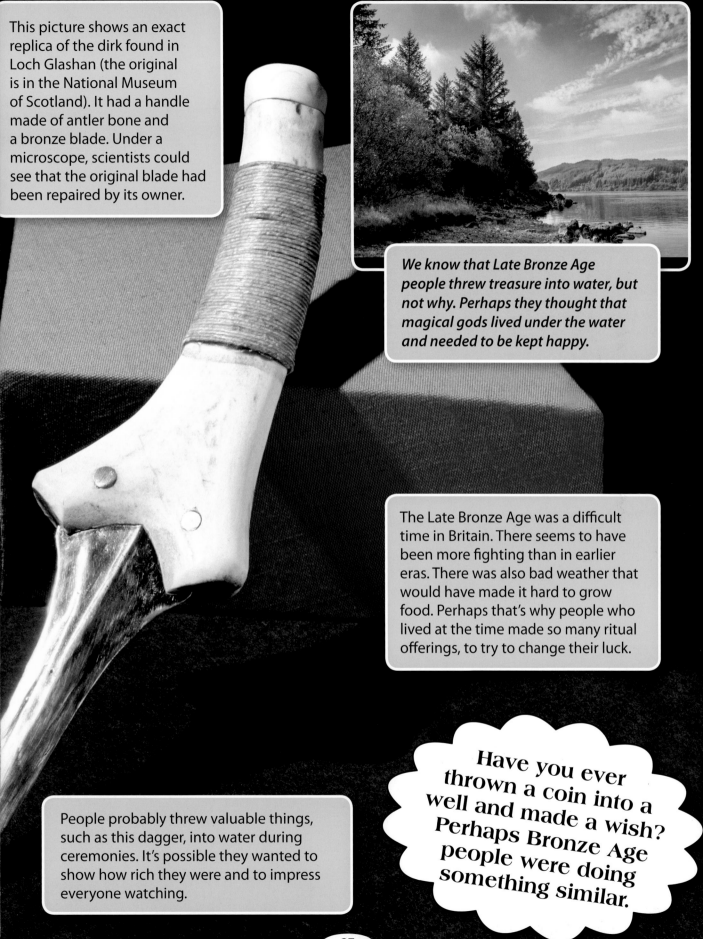

This picture shows an exact replica of the dirk found in Loch Glashan (the original is in the National Museum of Scotland). It had a handle made of antler bone and a bronze blade. Under a microscope, scientists could see that the original blade had been repaired by its owner.

We know that Late Bronze Age people threw treasure into water, but not why. Perhaps they thought that magical gods lived under the water and needed to be kept happy.

The Late Bronze Age was a difficult time in Britain. There seems to have been more fighting than in earlier eras. There was also bad weather that would have made it hard to grow food. Perhaps that's why people who lived at the time made so many ritual offerings, to try to change their luck.

People probably threw valuable things, such as this dagger, into water during ceremonies. It's possible they wanted to show how rich they were and to impress everyone watching.

Have you ever thrown a coin into a well and made a wish? Perhaps Bronze Age people were doing something similar.

For a fine warrior
MOEL HEBOG SHIELD

Towards the end of the Bronze Age people gathered together in tribes and fought each other for land. Warriors became more powerful in Britain, and some of them became chieftains, leading their tribes. They had fine armour made for them, such as the beautiful Moel Hebog shield discovered in a Welsh bog.

Around
1,000 BCE
LATE
BRONZE AGE

DATE FOUND:
1784, BY SOMEONE COLLECTING PEAT.

PLACE FOUND:
MOEL HEBOG,
SNOWDONIA, GWYNEDD.

When the shield was found it was in perfect condition and had never been used in battle. It might have been for show, held by a wealthy and important warrior during ceremonies. It was probably thrown into the bog as an offering, like the dagger on p. 26. Perhaps it was even made specifically

The shield was beaten into shape from one single disk of bronze. It has a central raised piece called a boss, surrounded by a design of rings. A bronze handle was riveted onto the back.

In the Late Bronze Age, metalworkers were becoming very skilled at making large bronze objects. Soon they would learn to make weapons and tools from iron, a much stronger metal. The period we call the Iron Age was about to begin.

The Bronze Age may have been a relatively peaceful era compared to what came next! The Iron Age was a warlike time, when tribes built hill forts such as Maiden Castle in Dorset, shown here.

Other very fine Late Bronze Age ceremonial treasures have been found in Britain and Ireland. For example, two beautiful gold armlets (bracelets) were discovered in an Irish bog at Derringboy in Ireland. It's thought they might have belonged to a warrior, too.

Do you think you would have made a good, farmer, potter, weaver, metal-maker or a fisherman during the Bronze Age?

Glossary

afterlife   The belief that the dead go to a place where they exist in a different life.

amber   Orange-coloured fossilised tree resin.

archaeologist   Someone who studies bones and man-made remains from the past.

armlet   A bracelet worn high on the arm.

barley   A type of cereal grain.

barrow   A burial chamber built from stones and covered with a mound of earth.

boss   The centre of a shield.

cereal crops   Plants grown for their edible grains, such as barley and wheat.

charcoal   Lumps of burnt wood that burn hotter than ordinary wood.

cist   A stone-lined, box-shaped grave.

copper ore   Rock containing copper.

creek   A narrow, sheltered inlet or channel filled with water.

cremated   When a body is burnt after death, usually in a ceremony.

cushion stone   A stone that acted as a Bronze Age metalworker's anvil.

fen   A watery, plant-filled marsh.

hill fort   A settlement on a hilltop with defensive earth walls and ditches around it.

ingot   A brick-shaped bar made of metal.

Iron Age   The period of history that came after the Bronze Age. It was a time when tools and weapons were made of iron.

molecule   A tiny part of something.

paddock   A small field or enclosure where animals are kept.

peat   Dense, brown, partly-decomposed vegetation, which can be burned as fuel.

plant fibres   Thin strings of plant material.

quill   The hard, central part of a bird's feather. It can be carved into a sharp point at the end, to use as a tool.

ritual   A series of actions performed in a certain order, usually at a ceremony.

roundhouse   A round home with a cone-shaped roof.

standing stone   A large stone placed upright in the landscape, perhaps to mark a special location.

stilts   A set of wooden posts that raise a building off the ground, often to avoid building on wet or boggy ground.

Stone Age   A time when early humans living on Earth used stone tools. They had not yet learnt how to make bronze.

Stonehenge   A huge monument in Wiltshire, made of circles of banks, ditches and standing stones that was built during the Late Stone Age and Early Bronze Age.

territory   An area of land belonging to someone.

tin   A silvery-coloured metal used to make bronze.

transom   A piece of wood fitted across the back of a boat.

tribe   A community of people, usually linked by family or by living close together.

Further Information

WEBLINKS

http://www.greatormemines.info/tour/
See a video of copper being smelted, as it was in the Bronze Age.

http://www.bbc.co.uk/programmes/p01zfx8k
See an animation of British life in the Bronze Age.

http://www.ancientcraft.co.uk/Archaeology/bronze-age/bronzeage_food.html
Try some Bronze Age food recipes.

Note to parents and teachers: Every effort has been made by the Publishers to ensure that the websites in this book are suitable for children, that they are of the highest educational value, and that they contain no inappropriate or offensive material. However, because of the nature of the Internet, it is impossible to guarantee that the contents of these sites will not be altered. We strongly advise that Internet access is supervised by a responsible adult.

TIMELINE

2,300 BCE   The start of the Early Bronze Age. Around this time the secrets of making bronze arrived in Britain. There were lots of ceremonial circle monuments around the country.

2,300 BCE   The Amesbury Archer was buried with the earliest gold items so far found in Britain.

2,200–1,500 BCE   Around this time the Boscombe Bowmen were buried near Stonehenge.

2,200–1,500 BCE   Around this time the Gardom's Edge carvings were made. People lived in roundhouses in small family groups. The Mold Cape was buried in a barrow.

1,400 BCE   The beginning of the Middle Bronze Age, when farms with fields developed. People were no longer buried in barrows. Instead their cremated remains were put into pots and buried in cemeteries.

1,000–700 BCE   A time known as the Late Bronze Age. A fleet of boats was deliberately sunk near Peterborough. Valuable objects were thrown into rivers and lakes as offerings. People lived on a platform over a river at Must Farm.

1,000–700 BCE   A ruling class of wealthy warriors seems to have developed.

700 BCE   Around this time the secret of making iron arrived in Britain. The period we call the Iron Age began, when hill forts were built for the first time.

INDEX

These are the lists of contents for titles in the FOUND! series:

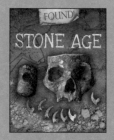

Also in the series:

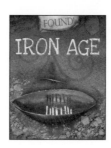